CONTENTS

KT-226-256

THE GREEK LANDSCAPE

The home of the ancient Greeks is a land of islands, sea, mountains and fast-flowing rivers. It is a land of brilliant light, with sun for 300 days a year. The Greeks farmed this land wherever they could. On the hills they looked after goats and sheep. And they sailed to and fro amongst the islands, fishing, trading and fighting.

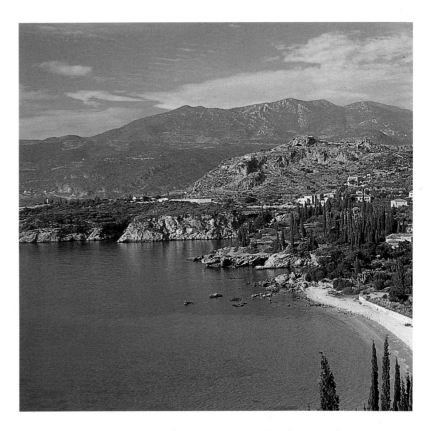

The ancient Greeks lived in a landscape of rocky coasts and high mountains.

This map shows the important cities of ancient Greece. Places in *italic* were religious centres, the others city-states.

The city-states

By about 800 BC many Greeks were living in communities known as city-states, each a town with some land around it. Each city-state looked after its own affairs with its own coins, its own laws, and so on.

Athens was the biggest city in Greece. Inside its city-state territory, called Attica, lived about 250,000 people. Athens was a centre of learning and new ideas and its influence was felt throughout the Greek world. The military state of Sparta was Athens' only real rival.

THE WORLD OF ANCIENT GREECE

EVERYDAY LIFE

ROBERT HULL

FRANKLIN WATTS

LONDON • SYDNEY

This edition 2003
Franklin Watts, 96 Leonard Street,
London EC2A 4XD

Franklin Watts Australia
45-51 Huntley Street,
Alexandria, NSW 2015

Copyright © Franklin Watts 1999

Series editor: Rachel Cooke
Designer: White Design
Consultant: Dr Anne Millard
Picture research: Susan Mennell
Artwork: Peter Bull Associates

A CIP catalogue record for this book
is available from the British Library.

ISBN 0 7496 5039 7

Dewey Decimal Classifaction: 938

Printed in Dubai U.A.E.

Acknowledgements:
Cover images: AKG (bl and br); E.T Archive (t)

AKG London pp. 2-3, 15b (John Hios), 8t, 8b,
9b, 11b, 12, 16t, 17t, 19b, 21t, 22-23, 26l,
26r, 28b, 29b (Erich Lessing/Musée du Louvre,
Paris), 9t (Erich Lessing/Musée Vivenel,
Compiegne), 13b (Erich Lessing/Museum of
Fine Arts, Boston), 14 (Erich Lessing/Museo
Nazionale Romano delle Terme), 15m (Erich
Lessing/National Museum of Archeology,
Naples), 19t, 20t, 28t (Erich
Lessing/Kunsthistoriches Museum, Vienna),25t
(Berlin, SMPK, Antikenmuseum) 20b; Ancient
Art and Architecture Collection pp. 5, 6, 6-7,
11t, 18, 25b, 27b; British Museum, London
pp. 14-15 (GR1920-12-21.1), 16b (GR1910-
6-15.4), 17b (806);
E.T. Archive pp. 24t (Archeological Museum,
Dion, Greece), 24b (Archeological Museum,
Salonica, Greece), 27t (Acropolis Archive
Museum, Athens); Eye Ubiquitous pp. 4 (Bob
Gibbons), 23b (Anna Barry), 19m, 29t (Julia
Waterlow); Robert Harding pp. 13t, 22;
Robert Hull p. 23t; Rex Features p. 7.

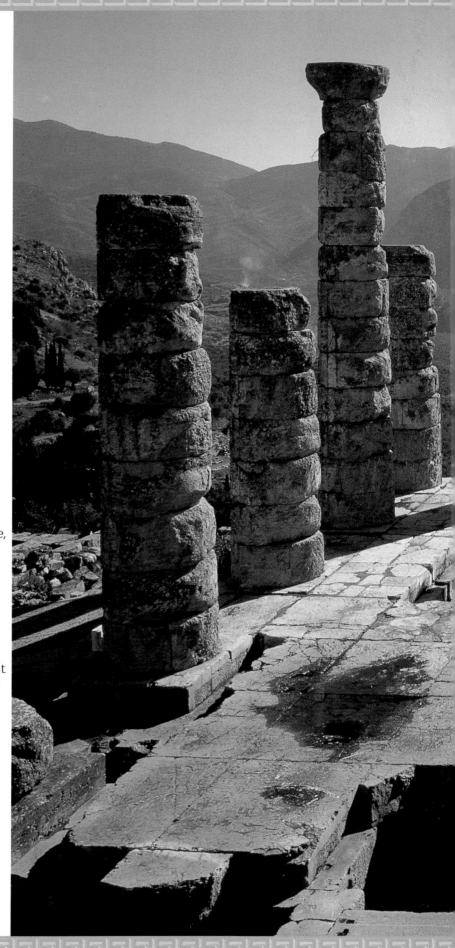

Colonies

The Greeks also began setting up new communities — colonies — outside Greece. Some founded cities on the coast of what is now Turkey. Others went to Sicily and other parts of the Mediterranean.

Despite the separate states and colonies, the Greeks had many things in common — one Greek writer, Herodotus, described it in this way: 'We are all Greek. We have the same language, the same gods and temples and way of life.'

EUROPE

SCYTHIA

GAUL

BLACK SEA

Massilia

Emporiae

Sinope

IBERIA

Saguntum

Byzantium

ASIA

Cumae

Taras

Sparta

Ephesus

Syracuse

Athens

Cydonia

PHOENICIA

MEDITERRANEAN SEA

■ COLONIES

Cyrene

Naucratis

AFRICA

EGYPT

This map shows the areas of the Mediterranean colonized by the ancient Greeks.

history: This is a book about Greek history. The word 'history' comes from a Greek word *istoria*, which means discoveries.

■■■ LEGACY ■■■ ■■

We know about the ancient Greeks because of what they left behind: their temples and stadiums, and the everyday things like vases and toys that archaeologists have dug up. The Greek legacy is more than this — we can still read their philosophers, poets and historians and share their legends and myths. Their plays are still performed in our theatres and many of the words they used have become part of our language.

This ancient Greek vase shows men beating and shaking olives from a tree. Olives are still sometimes harvested like this today.

When was Greece ancient?

Greek history dates back far earlier than the city-states, with the Mycenaean civilization emerging in about 1700 BC. It continues through a time when Greece was controlled by rulers like Alexander the Great and the Roman emperors. However, the time of the city-states, which lasted about 450 years, is the main focus of this book (around 800 to 350 BC).

CITIZENS

The ancient Greek city-state is sometimes called a citizen-state. This is because, by the 5th century BC, citizens in some cities came together to make important decisions for the state, like whether to go to war, or found a new colony.

These 'ballots' were used by jury members to show if they judged someone innocent or guilty.

THEIR OWN WORDS

'Our way of governing is a model to others. It is called democracy, because the majority manage its affairs, not just a few; …when we pick someone for public office, what counts is his personal ability, not whether he belongs to a particular class…'

Pericles, an Athenian leader in 431 BC, as reported by the historian Thucydides.

This is the platform in Athens where citizens stood to give speeches to the Assembly.

Who was a citizen?

Each city-state had their own rules about who was a citizen. Athenian citizenship was for Athenian-born men and women who were not slaves or foreigners (which included other Greeks). Only men could vote and make laws. Occasionally, non-Athenians became citizens but this was rare. In some other states, only wealthy people could be citizens, so the state was really ruled by very few people.

politics: We get our word 'politics' from the Greek word for city-state – *polis*.

Rule by the people

In Athens any male citizen over 20 could speak at the citizen meeting, called the Assembly. Then they voted, by holding up hands, or sticks. The government was by 'the people' not by others elected to represent them. In addition, men over 30 had to serve as jury-members in the law-courts. The Athenians called their government a democracy.

Former US President Clinton and President Mandela of South Africa were both leaders of democratic governments.

Most countries today describe the way they are ruled as a democracy, based on the ideas that began in ancient Athens. There have been many developments since then. For example, rather than every single citizen being involved in every decision, citizens vote for people to represent them in parliament. And voting citizens are not just men, but women as well. It is also far easier for a foreigner to become a citizen.

Councils

Most city-states had a council that prepared laws for the Assembly to discuss. In Athens the 500-man Council was made up of citizens over 30. Councillors only served for a year, and they were all chosen by lot. The Council's role was to help the Assembly work better.

But in other states the Council really controlled the Assembly. In Sparta, Athens' main rival, and at times its enemy, the Council was made up of men over 60, chosen for life; and they were under the influence of powerful officials and, strangely enough, two kings.

SLAVES AND NON-CITIZENS

Slaves were part of Greek life. When Athens' population was about 250,000, at least 75,000 were slaves. The philosopher Aristotle said the slave was simply 'a living tool'. Only the very poor went without slaves, and very rich families might have 50 each.

A row of female slaves make bread.

Who were slaves?

Many slaves were servants – porter, nurse, tutor, goat-herd or bee-keeper – and, as such, part of the Greek household. Slaves even went with their owners to war. Other slaves worked in crafts and industry.

Slaves might be born and bred to slavery in a household. Free people might become slaves when they were captured in war, or kidnapped, or found when 'exposed' as babies (see page 16). Very poor people might be forced to become slaves to clear their debts.

In Athens

Athenians believed that slaves should be well-treated – one surprised visitor complained, 'in Athens, it is not permitted to strike slaves'. Even so, by law, slaves suspected of a crime or giving evidence at a trial were tortured. In the silver mines away from the city, slaves worked in narrow tunnels, on their hands and knees. Above ground they were often chained.

An old slave nurses a child. Figurines like this were often left as offerings at temple shrines.

8

In Sparta

In Sparta, there were fewer citizens and many more slaves. When Sparta conquered next-door Messenia, the Messenians became Spartan slaves. They lived in their own country, with their own possessions, but as subjects of Sparta — *helots*. They had to serve in the Spartan army, and give up half their crops. 'In Sparta a slave is really a slave,' the saying went.

Prisoners captured by soldiers in war often became their slaves.

THEIR OWN WORDS

'Thrasyboulous proposed the motion that the foreigners who helped in the return … should have citizenship … they stood by the demos, and did what was ordered.'

An inscription from 410 BC declaring citizen status had been given to 1000 *metics* who helped the people protect Athens against an attempted take-over. The *metics'* occupations are listed: donkey-driver, statue-maker, gardener, and so on.

Other non-citizens

Many non-Greeks were attracted to Greek cities, particularly Athens. These foreigners were called *metics*. They did not have citizen status but could own businesses and slaves themselves, and sometimes became citizens. They included factory-owners, like Lysias, who made shields, and Aspasia, a woman who trained young girls to entertain at men's dinner parties.

A worker feeds the flames of a pottery kiln. Potteries were often owned by *metics*.

9

HOUSE AND HOME

A Greek house faced in on itself. The outside walls were plain, with tiny windows, but the house came to life through the entrance way, beyond the dust and glare of the street, in a central open-air courtyard.

The 'best' room where men ate and drank.

Stairs to women's quarters and bedrooms.

The main work rooms, including kitchen.

Around the courtyard

The main rooms opened on to the courtyard, which was designed so as not to be seen from the street, and was usually south-facing. It generally had a veranda with a small colonnade and a family altar, and perhaps a shady fig tree. Even small houses had a courtyard; larger ones had two.

All the downstairs rooms opened on to the courtyard.

Roofs were covered with pottery tiles.

Windows were small and often shuttered.

Walls were stone-based with mud brick on top.

Well-off families had a slave-porter at the entrance.

This is a reconstruction of a farmhouse. The plan above shows the layout of the rooms.

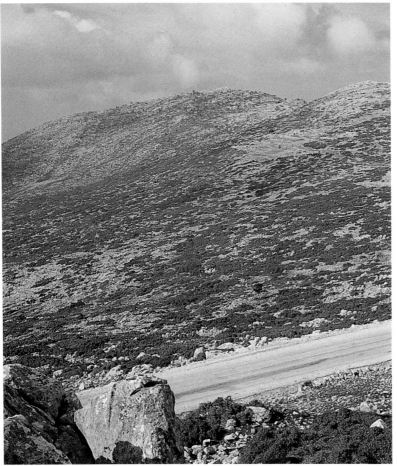

In parts of Greece like this, where trees were scarce, timber was highly valued.

domestic: The Greek word for house was *domos*, which in Latin became *domus*. These words gave us 'domestic', which means to do with the home.

Furniture

There was not much furniture in Greek houses. They had boxes and chests for storing things like clothes, and low three-legged tables for food. Ordinary houses had simple stools; richer people had couches and elegant chairs, with seats of leather or fibre cords.

Building materials

Houses were mostly erected on stone foundations, and built of dry mud brick strengthened with timber. Wood and mud brick do not last, so there are few remains of private Greek houses. But some large farmhouses have been excavated, revealing pottery roof tiles and flagstones that probably paved the courtyard. Remains of smaller houses suggest very cramped living spaces, with some built directly into rocky hillsides.

Houses had wooden doors, balconies and shutters to keep out the summer heat. In some areas wood was scarce and therefore valuable – during a war between Athens and Sparta, some people who fled the fighting even took their doors and shutters with them.

A young woman sits on a wooden chair doing her hair. Unusually for a Greek vase painting, she looks directly at you.

FAMILY LIFE

The family was the centre of Greek life. Their word for family – *oikos* – meant not just the people living in the house, but their land, buildings, slaves, animals, farm-implements, graves, and so on. Each family had a male head, and when he died the family land was divided between his sons – who then started their own *oikos*.

economy: Our word economy, which we use to describe the managing of money, comes from the ancient Greek word *oikonomia* – meaning managing the house or family.

The task of spinning wool and weaving cloth was women's work.

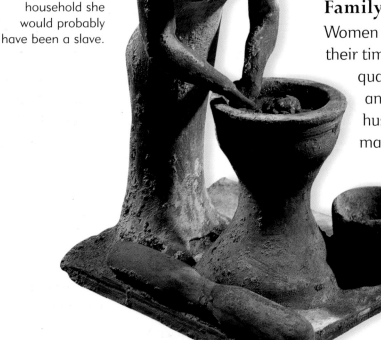

A woman makes bread. In a richer, household she would probably have been a slave.

Family work

Women managed the house, and spent most of their time inside it. They had their own quarters, which were sometimes upstairs and out of bounds to any man except a husband or close relative. There they made the family's clothing, and the hangings and coverings for beds and couches. They also supervised the cooking and cleaning – or did it themselves – and looked after the children and the house slaves.

Out of the house

Women from poor families might work, perhaps in the market selling vegetables, but normally it was only if the family couldn't afford slaves that women left the house to fetch water, or do the shopping. Women went to funerals and weddings, and public festivals, and they might pop out to borrow some salt, or see the new baby. But mostly they stayed in.

LEGACY

In many parts of modern Greece, there are cafés *(kafenion)* which women rarely visit. These men-only cafés are perhaps a legacy of men and women's separate living quarters in ancient Greece.

THEIR OWN WORDS

'You won't allow us to leave the house, or even peep out of the door; And if ever you find that your wife is out, you bellow, you rage and you roar... She may have been paying a neighbourly call, on a woman who's just had a son.'

A woman in *The Poet and the Women*, a play by Aristophanes, complains about being trapped at home.

Separate lives

Men spent their working hours – if they worked – in the fields or workshops. Otherwise they could be at the *gymnasion*, the Assembly, the jury-court or chatting in the barber's-shop! Men were expected to be busy, but not usually at home. Sparta took this one step further: men ate all their meals in army barracks. Their role as soldiers was more important than that of family men.

Laundry was another task left exclusively to women.

13

WOMEN AS WIVES

Women in ancient Greece were not independent. They were protected and controlled by a male guardian: first their father, then their husband and later still their son. They could not own property, except for clothes, jewels and slaves, but in Sparta some women owned land. Even as citizens, they could not vote.

Marriage

Girls married young, often at 13 or 14. The husband was often older, 30 or more. Parents arranged the marriage. In the engagement ceremony the woman's father 'gave her away', transferring her from his family to her future husband's. The engagement was a business matter, agreeing on the size of the bride's dowry (the gift from her father). Sometimes, the bride did not meet her husband till the day of the wedding.

The wedding

Before the wedding, the bride dedicated gifts — like her childhood toys — to the goddess Artemis, protector of girls. On the day itself, the house of her parents was hung with garlands, and an animal sacrifice was made. After the marriage feast, as in the painted scene above, the couple drove to the groom's house, and the wedding guests followed. The bride's mother held a torch, taking fire from her daughter's old home to her new one.

A veiled bride burns incense as a sacrifice before her wedding.

THEIR OWN WORDS

An admiring Roman painted this picture of the poetess Sappho 800 years after she died. But Greek men did not see women as their equals.

The ability to think is not present in slaves; it does not work in women ... the male is by nature superior.

The philosopher Aristotle

Once women were married

Women could divorce men, but men often resisted, because they had to give back the dowry. Women could be divorced easily; they were simply returned to their original family. A husband even had the legal right to kill a wife if he found her with a lover.

Within marriage, women ran the household and some achieved fame, such as the poetess Sappho. Women also served as priestesses in some temples, and there was once a woman warship captain, Artemisia.

The ruins of the temple of Apollo, god of prophecy, at Delphi. People came to Delphi to find out the future from the priestess, through whom Apollo spake.

15

CHILDREN

Childhood in ancient Greece was full of toys and games, but before this a new baby had a frightening start to life.

A dark beginning

When a baby was born, the father inspected it to see if it was healthy. A baby who was at all deformed, or just very weak, could be 'exposed' — left in a public place, either to die or be rescued, perhaps by a slave.

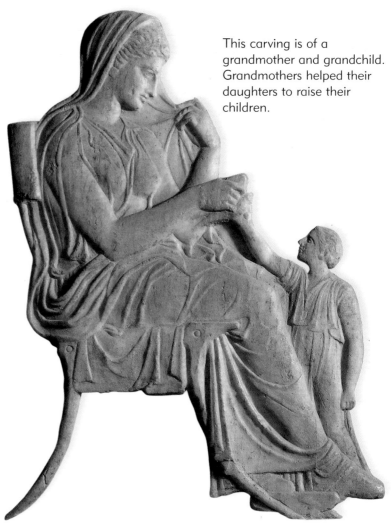

This carving is of a grandmother and grandchild. Grandmothers helped their daughters to raise their children.

In Sparta, babies were the soldiers — or the mothers of soldiers — of the future. State officials decided whether a new-born baby was strong enough. Weaklings were tossed over a cliff. In the rest of Greece, the father decided. The baby who passed his fit-to-live test was accepted into the family, and given a name — often that of the father's parents.

As well as those who were exposed, many Greek babies died naturally. Probably only about half of the children born to Greek families actually survived to the age of 18.

This child on a potty — waving a rattle and perhaps shouting, 'Finished!' — is painted on a small wine-jug.

A normal childhood

There is plenty of archaeological evidence to tell us about childhood games. In painting and sculpture little ones play with rattles and dolls, doll-sized furniture and pots and pans, and little two-wheeled carts. Older children play with tops, kites, yo-yos, see-saws, and swings, or they bowl hoops or sit fishing.

A child plays on a 'horse': a stick with a wheel at its end.

Greek children were told stories about heroes, gods, animals, ghosts and so on. Their pets were tortoises, dogs, geese and hens — though not cats. Dogs and goats in toy harness pulled their little carts.

Until they were about six boys and girls were brought up and taught together at home. After that, boys went off to school; girls did their learning at home.

Toy animals, like this terracotta goose with a boy rider, were popular with Greek children.

paediatrician: We get the English word 'paediatrician', a doctor who specializes in children's illnesses, from the Greek *paidion*, meaning a child.

LEARNING AND SCHOOL

Greek laws said that parents had to educate children, but city-states did not build state schools. Schools were private, for boys whose parents could afford them.

Future citizens

Girls did not go to school but were educated at home and learnt how to manage a household. Boys were trained to be citizens. By the 5th century BC, Greek male citizens had to be able to read notices and write laws. They had to sing and dance at feasts and festivals. So boys learned how to read and write, how to dance and play an instrument. They learned lots of poetry too – by heart; and simple maths.

Some girls were taught to read although they did not go to school.

LEGACY

The Greeks 'imported' their alphabet in the 8th century, from the Phoenicians; they called the letters *Phoenikia* – Phoenician things. Writing spread quickly, and by the 5th century male citizens were expected to read and write. The Romans later adapted the Greek alphabet for their written language and this is the alphabet we use today. Our word alphabet comes from *alpha* and *beta*, the first two letters of the Greek alphabet.

A	a	N	n
B	b	Ξ	x
Γ	g	O	o
Δ	d	Π	p
E	e	P	r, rh
Z	z	Σ	s
H	e	T	t
Θ	th	Y	y, u
I	i	Φ	ph
K	c,k	X	ch
Λ	l	Ψ	ps
M	m	Ω	o

grammar: Do you study grammar at school? Our word 'grammar' comes from the Greek *gramma*, meaning writing.

Training the body

Boys were trained for the army, which was made up of citizens. They learnt boxing, wrestling, running and so on, at a *palaestra* with trained coaches. Boys exercised naked, which shocked foreigners.

Boys stayed at school until they were 15. Then they continued at a *gymnasion*, a large sports centre with a running track. In Athens, young men of 18 spent two years doing military training there.

Boxing was always popular in ancient Greece. This vase painting shows a man binding his hands before a fight.

We still train our bodies and run races. But trainers do not carry whips, as they often did in ancient Greece!

Gymnastics for the mind

Because the *gymnasion* was where young men gathered, it was there that travelling teachers gave lectures on history, science, philosophy, maths and so on. Famous teachers set up colleges. Plato's Academy and Aristotle's Lyceum became the first 'universities' in Europe.

In schools, boys wrote on a re-usable wax tablet, carving letters with the thin end of a stylus. The broad end smoothed out any mistakes.

A Spartan education

In Sparta, boys of 12 went to live in military barracks, and lived there until they were 30. They slept in the open air and had to go barefoot. Part of their education was the 'experience of going hungry'. The aim was to produce brave soldiers, loyal to the state. Spartan girls had physical training too so that as mothers they would produce strong children.

19

LEISURE TIME

With slaves and *metics* doing much of the everyday work in ancient Greece, citizens had plenty of leisure time.

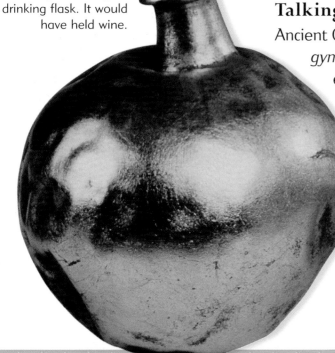

A huntsman sets out with his dog on a lead.

Hunting

Hunting was a favourite rich men's pastime in early Greece. Men rode – without stirrups or saddle – to hunt hare, deer and wild boar. They hunted on foot, too, with their dogs, and raced horses.

The Greeks had animals as pets; a character in a play says that he would like some pet pheasants, perhaps a heron. But the Greeks also enjoyed cock-fights, between quail or partridge for instance. They even fed them garlic before a fight to 'liven them up'.

A replica of a gold drinking flask. It would have held wine.

Talking

Ancient Greeks loved to talk! After a few hours at the *gymnasion*, there would be news and gossip to exchange in public places around the city. Some of the philosopher Socrates' conversations were held at Simon the Cobbler's workshop. In the evening there was the drinking-party – the *symposion* – in the men's dining room of private houses. Guests lay on couches, served by female slaves. The wine-drinking came after the meal. There was discussion, poetry and song. Everyone recited and sang. Drinking games were also popular.

THEIR OWN WORDS

In *The Wasps*, a comedy by Aristophanes, Procleon advised on how to behave at a *symposion*. He has climbed onto a couch: *Just recline, gracefully.* [Procleon lies flat on his back, knees in the air.] *Not like that! Straighten your knees, now pour yourself back into the cushions with a sinuous athletic grace.* [P. practises pouring himself into the cushions.] *Now you gaze round, up at the ceiling, admire the hanging rugs, the bronze ornaments…*

A guest at a *symposion* pours himself back into the cushions.

These girls are playing knucklebones. They toss a bone and try to pick up others before catching it. It is like our game of jacks.

Women's leisure

Wives did not attend *symposia*. Women do not seem to have had the leisure that men had. But they had plenty of opportunity to gossip and play games in the home. One sculpture shows girls playing knucklebones, a game like jacks, which involved throwing small animal bones in the air and catching them. In Sparta — as usual — things were different and women were encouraged to exercise and move around as freely as men.

FARMING AND FOOD

Three main crops – cereals, olives and grapes – gave the Greeks their three vital foods. Their basic food was bread from wheat and barley. Olive trees gave them olives for the table, and precious oil for cooking, lighting, washing, and even perfume. And grapes gave them their usual drink, wine.

diet: Our word for what we eat, our 'diet', comes from the Greek word *diaita*, which means way of life.

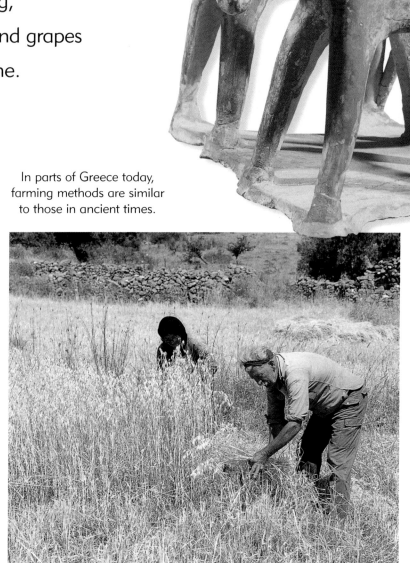

In parts of Greece today, farming methods are similar to those in ancient times.

Growing crops

The Greeks adapted wild olive trees and tended them in groves. They often grew corn between fruit trees – fig, apple, pomegranate, plum, and others. The smaller vines were free-standing, but others were propped on stakes or draped on trees. Greek farmers also grew crops like beans and lentils, celery, parsley, onions, leeks and garlic.

Eating at home

Greek meals usually had bread as the main item, with tasty side-dishes like olives, leeks, cheese and fish. They ate only a little meat, mainly pork and lamb. Rearing animals was expensive, so meat was mainly for festivals.

Unlike meat, fish could always be bought in the market. Writers talk of 'fish-gluttons', including one who nearly died eating a whole metre-long octopus!

With such a long coastline, fishing has always been a part of Greek life.

This 7th-century BC figurine shows a farmer with his plough and team.

■■■ LEGACY ■■■

Our modern diet includes foods that have been handed down or borrowed from the Greeks: wine, olives, figs and feta cheese. In some parts of Greece people still tend to eat meat at religious festivals, like lamb at Easter, and even sometimes to allocate certain parts to the priests, as in ancient times.

Farm animals

The Greek countryside was full of animal-sounds: donkeys, mules, cattle, pigs, horses, geese, hens, and − on the hillside − goats, sheep, and bees. Honey from hives was the Greek sweetener. From his animals the Greek farmer had milk and cheeses (but no butter!), meat and eggs. They also gave him transport and tons of manure.

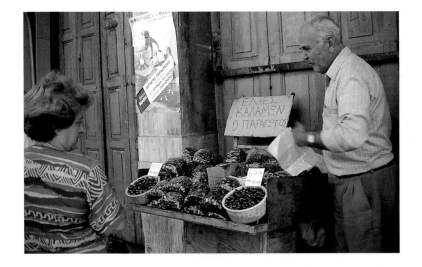

Kalamata olives, much-prized in ancient Greece, on sale in Athens today

CRAFT AND INDUSTRY

The ancient Greeks had busy workshops and factories. They made ships, bricks, pots, beehives, drainpipes, coins, tables, jewellery, sports equipment, armaments and many other things.

This gold wreath of ivy leaves shows the skill of the Greek goldsmiths.

A centre of craft

Athens was the busiest city, full of craftsmen from all over the Greek world. An old law said that citizens had to teach their sons a trade, but Athenian craftsmen were mostly *metics* and slaves. There were whole streets of small craft shops, and a Potters' Quarter – the *Kerameikos*. There was a mint in one corner of the *agora*, or market place, in Athens.

Athens had factories, too. The largest – Lysias' shield factory – employed 120 slaves. One factory making couches had 20 slaves workers. But small workshops of four or five workers were more common. Smaller communities also had their own craftsmen, such as blacksmiths and carpenters.

This gold quiver for arrows belonged to Philip of Macedonia. Armour was made for show as well as battle.

technology: Our words 'technology' and 'technique' come from the Greek *techne*, meaning craft or skill.

Workers mine clay for pottery. This tablet was a dedication left at a shrine near the potteries of Athens.

Rebuilding Athens

Greek cities were full of temples and public buildings, statues and tombstones. But especially in the 5th century, when much of Athens was rebuilt after a war, stone-carvers, sculptors, painters, carpenters and others were in great demand. As were workers in bronze, when hollow bronze sculptures became fashionable. The bronzes were light to carry, and didn't break.

The raw materials

All these trades depended on workers in mines, quarries, logging camps, and so on. Traces can still be found of the work of the men who produced the lead and silver needed to keep Greece prosperous. The fleet that defeated the Persians in a 5th-century war was paid for by a find of silver, in Laurion, south of Athens. Thousands of slaves and hundreds of free men worked the mines in dangerous conditions, carrying a chisel and an oil-lamp.

Blacksmiths work at a furnace. One holds tongs, the other works the bellows.

CLOTHES AND JEWELLERY

Greek looms wove wool cloth in rectangular pieces. Greek women folded and pinned or sewed these squares in different ways to make the two main Greek garments — the *chiton* and *himation*.

This woman wears a *chiton*, the man wears a *himation*.

Chiton and *himation*

The *chiton* was wrapped round the body, and pinned in various ways at the shoulder. Women wore it to the ankle; men and children — and dancers — to the knee. The *himation* went over the *chiton* in cool weather.

Men often wore white, but brown for working in the fields or workshops. Spartan men wore flowing red cloaks. Saffron yellow was popular for women.

A woman, dressed in a *chiton*, admires herself in a mirror. She holds her jewellery box in the other hand.

Hats and shoes

Normally most Greeks went bare-headed, but for travelling, or work, men had caps and hats. Fishermen and some craftsmen wore a conical cap, a *pilos*. Greek footwear was sandals — leather flip-flops — or soft boots reaching up the calf. Some women put cork in their shoes to be taller. Many people went barefoot in summer.

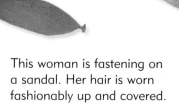

This woman is fastening on a sandal. Her hair is worn fashionably up and covered.

Hair styles

Women usually wore their hair long, and up, sometimes gathered into a net, scarf or cap. They decorated it with pins or ribbons.

Female slaves wore their hair short. So did men, too, after about the 5th century. But earlier, in the 6th century, men's hair was often long, and bound in place with gold. In Sparta, men continued to grow their hair as it was considered 'the mark of a gentleman'. Older men usually grew beards.

This boy's head was carved about 470 BC. His hair style is one popular at the time.

THEIR OWN WORDS

Perhaps because Greek clothes didn't have pockets, the Greeks carried loose change in the mouth. One character in *The Wasps* is tricked in the market this way:

They hadn't got the change, and we were given a drachma between us, and we went to the fish-market to change it. But what he put into my mouth were three fish-scales — ugh!

The Wasps, Aristophanes

Make-up and jewellery

Women used white lead (which was poisonous!) to keep the skin pale, and alkanet root to redden the cheeks. Less respectable women wore eye make-up. Otherwise women wore plenty of scent and some jewellery — ear-studs, bracelets and chains. Men wore rings, bangles and armbands. Finally, to make sure everything looked right, they used mirrors of polished bronze or silver.

Hidden in the delicate work of this earring is a figure playing a lyre.

HEALTH

In many ways Greeks lived healthy lives. They had a wonderful sunny climate and a diet that to us seems very sensible, with plenty of sport and exercise. But they did not have the same knowledge of medicine and hygiene we have today.

A man scrapes himself clean with a strigil.

A young woman washes and scrubs her feet.

Life spans

Greeks did not live as long as we do. Perhaps as many as 40 per cent of Greeks were under 18, and as few as 5 per cent over 60. Many teenagers had only one parent alive.

hygiene: The Greeks had a goddess of health, Hygeia. From her name comes our word 'hygiene'.

Sanitation

Only a few houses had a private water-supply. Water came mainly from public fountains or a well. Greeks washed in large pots, using sponges; they rubbed olive-oil in the skin, scraped it off with a strigil and splashed down with water. There was no proper sewage-disposal, only rubbish-collection.

A bad harvest could cause famine. At times, in war especially, disease and plague struck: during a long struggle against Sparta, half the people of Athens died of the plague.

The doctor Hippocrates is sometimes called the father of medicine. He wrote a Doctors' Oath – the Hippocratic Oath – which was used for centuries in Western Europe. It sounds modern: *I will use treatment to help the sick and never to cause harm... I will not give poison even though asked to do so... A doctor must not talk about what he discovers from a patient. Those things are holy secrets.* Doctors today are still not meant to reveal information about their patients – an idea learned from ancient Greece.

Perhaps because of diet and climate, Greeks today live longer than world averages.

Hippocrates studied at a medical school in Athens.

Medicine

The Greeks took a great interest in medicine. Writers like Hippocrates offered advice that stressed diet and lifestyle, and rest and exercise.

Some doctors were priests of Asclepius, the god of healing. Greeks needing cures went to the god's 'health-resorts', with temples, priests and hospitals. Others tried age-old magic methods. Hypnosis was used occasionally.

In some cities medical schools were set up. Surgeons and doctors from these schools sometimes worked for the state, for instance with the army in war. They were well paid. The ancient Greeks may not have understood illness and disease as well as we do, but their ideas are the foundation for medical teaching and practice today.

29

GLOSSARY

agora: a large open space in the centre of the town, a market-place or square.

Aristophanes (c. 450-385 BC): the most famous Greek writer of comedies. He made fun of several well-known politicians in fierce anti-war plays. His plays are very funny, and tell us a lot about Greek life.

Aristotle (384-322 BC): a famous philosopher and scientist. He observed and collected information very painstakingly, then classified it, and used it all to develop theories about many things.

Artemis: the goddess of the moon, hunting and protector of young girls.

Asclepius: a god of healing, who was also supposed to be able to bring the dead to life. He was worshipped at an *asclepium*, a sanctuary where people went to be cured.

Assembly: the group of male citizens who came together, or assembled, to make the decisions and laws that governed the state. The place where these meetings took place was also called the Assembly.

citizen: someone who really belonged to the city-state and had all the rights of citizens, unlike slaves and *metics*. In some states, to be a citizen both your parents had to be citizens. Both men and women were citizens, but only men could vote in the Assembly. In politics, women were 'second-class' citizens.

colonnade: a line of columns outside a covered-in walkway. In Greece, temples, market-places and courtyards in the home might all have colonnades.

colony: a settlement of people who have left their own homes to live somewhere else. After about 800 BC, Greek cities sent out many colonists, who were usually still citizens of the mother-state, or *metropolis*.

drachma: the unit in which Greek money is counted, both in ancient and modern Greece.

gymnasion: a kind of Greek sports centre, where athletes trained and exercised. Some gymnasia were large and very well equipped; others might be smaller. The gymnasion also became a place where teaching took place.

helot: a slave from Messenia, who served the Spartans, giving them farm produce, manual labour and military service.

TIMELINE

c. 1700 BC	Mycenaean civilization emerges.
c. 1200	Mycenaean palaces burnt.
c. 1200-800	'Dark Age' in Greece. Knowledge of writing lost.
c. 1100	Greeks migrate to Asian coast of Mediterranean: Ionia.
c. 1050	Iron in use for weapons and tools.
c. 1000-750	Phoenicians travel and trade around Mediterranean.
c. 800	Greek trading posts in Syria and Egypt.
c. 800-500	Greeks settling all round Mediterranean and Black Sea.
776	First all-Greece Olympic Games.
c. 750-700	Homer composes his long poems.
c. 750	Writing reintroduced to Greece. Also new heavy armour.
c. 700	Stone first used for temples.
c. 700	Athens combines with towns of Attica to make one city-state.
534	First Athenian drama festival.
520	First naked winner in Olympics.
507	Athens becomes a democracy.
493	Silver found in Laurium, Attica.
490	Greece invaded by Persia, Greek victory at Marathon.

Herodotus (c. 480-425 BC): sometimes called the first historian, Herodotus wrote about the wars between the Greeks and Persians that took place in his lifetime. He travelled all over the Greek world, collecting information about different peoples and customs.

Hippocrates (469-399 BC): the most famous Greek writer on medicine and healing. He looked for scientific explanations of illnesses at a time when many thought cures for disease came only from the gods.

Homer (c. 8th century BC): the blind poet who composed two great story-poems, *The Iliad* and *The Odyssey*, that were recited and performed in ancient Greece long after his death. They are still read today.

jury: in law, a group of people who decide at a trial whether someone is innocent or guilty of the crime he or she is charged with.

metic: a foreign resident in a Greek city-state, including Greeks from other states. Many *metics* worked as merchants and craftsmen.

mint: a factory where coins were made.

Mycenaean: describes the civilization that existed in Greece from around 1700 BC but seems to have collapsed about 500 years later. Many Greek stories and religious beliefs seem to have originated around this time.

oikos: the Greek family, including all the property in its possession.

palaestra: the sand wrestling ground that was a central feature of the *gymnasion*, although it it could be found on its own.

philosopher: a word meaning lover of wisdom. In schools and universities, we still study Greek philosophers, like Plato and Aristotle.

Phoenicians: a people from the eastern Mediterranean, who were very successful traders and travellers from about 1050 BC. The Greeks borrowed their alphabet and adapted it for their language.

Plato (c. 428-348 BC): a Greek philosopher whose writings and ideas are a major foundation of philosophy as it is studied today.

Sappho (c. 600 BC): the most famous of several well-known Greek woman poets.

Socrates (c. 470-399 BC): a Greek philosopher whose ideas were very influential in developing Greek thinking and methods of discussion. He wrote nothing down. We know of him through his friend, Plato.

symposion: the evening drinking party held for men in the men's dining room of private houses.

480	Athens burnt by Persians, Greeks win at Salamis.
479	Greeks win at Platea, Persians go home.
478	Athens forms the Federation of Delos, so becoming an empire.
c. 454	Pericles is a leader in Athens.
451	Pay for jury in law-courts begins.
447	Building of the Parthenon in Athens begins.

c. 445-426	Herodotus travelling and writing.
431-404	Peloponnesian War between Athens and Sparta.
c. 430	Hippocrates working on Cos.
429	Death of Pericles. Plague in Athens.
425	Aristophanes' first anti-war play produced.
404	Athens surrenders to Sparta

399	Socrates forced to take poison by the Athenian Assembly.
384	Birth of Aristotle.
359-338	Philip II becomes King of Macedon and conquers the rest of Greece.
336-323	His son, Alexander the Great, rules. His armies conquer large areas of Asia.
323	Death of Alexander.

INDEX